THE POWER OF EVERYDAY
STEM

TURNING DAILY ACTIVITIES
INTO LEARNING ADVENTURES

Miss Sierra

ISBN 978-1-959451-81-5

Siohan Press
www.siohanpress.com

Contents

THE POWER OF EVERYDAY STEM

Part I:

The STEM Mindset

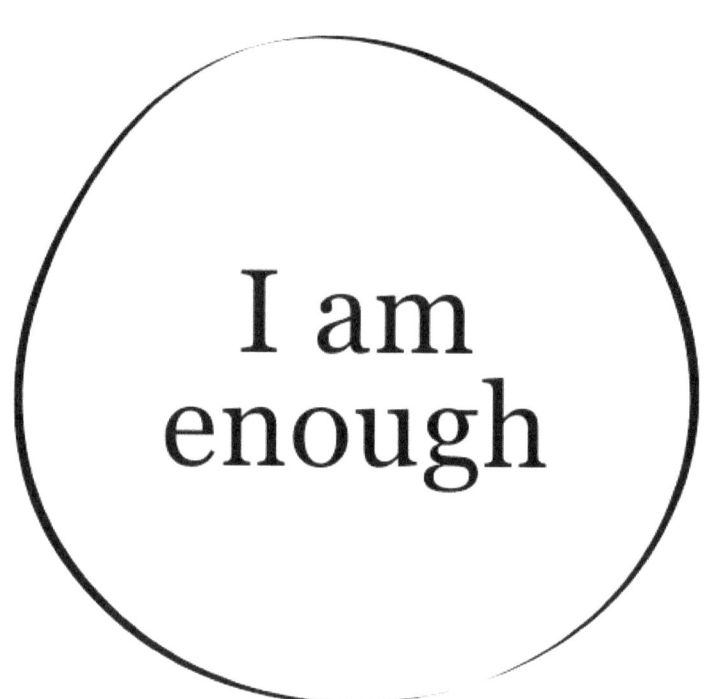

The Power of Everyday STEM

Introduction: STEM is Everywhere

Right now, as you read this, your child is learning science, technology, engineering, and math. Maybe they're watching you sort laundry or asking questions about the car. They could be helping you cook dinner. They might be playing with blocks in the living room.

Every single day, you show your child how the world works. You don't need special training. You don't need expensive materials. You don't need to be good at math or science. You are already the perfect STEM teacher for your child.

This book will help you see what you're already doing right.

This is not a book about turning your home into a classroom. This is not about making your child study more. This is about recognizing the incredible learning that already happens during your normal day.

When you drive to the store, they experience physics. When you pay bills, they watch mathematics. When you fix something that's broken, they observe engineering. When you make breakfast, your child sees chemistry.

Your everyday routines are full of STEM learning. You just need to notice it. This book helps you recognize and build on what's working.

Many STEM books focus on special activities and experiments. This book focuses on what you're already doing. You already have everything you need.

Why Everyday STEM Matters

Children learn best when they see how knowledge connects to real life. Math makes sense when they help measure ingredients. Science becomes interesting when they watch ice melt in their drinks. Engineering feels important when they help you solve problems around the house.

Everyday STEM requires:

- Noticing what's already happening
- Pointing out interesting things you see
- Asking simple questions together
- Following your child's natural curiosity
- Using whatever is already around you

The Power of Everyday STEM

Everyday STEM helps children:

- See that learning happens everywhere, not just in school
- Understand that they can figure things out on their own
- Build confidence in asking questions and trying new ideas
- Connect what they learn to what they care about

Everyday STEM helps families:

- Spend quality time together while learning
- Use materials you already have at home
- Make the most of time you're already spending together
- Build strong foundations without extra pressure or expense

Most importantly, everyday STEM shows children that they belong in the world of science, technology, engineering, and math. These subjects aren't just for other people. They're for everyone.

You don't need to be a teacher to help your child learn. You don't need to know all the answers. You just need to be curious together.

Your job is to:

- Notice interesting things happening around you
- Point out cool discoveries you make together
- Ask "What do you think?" and "What do you notice?"
- Follow your child's questions and interests
- Stay curious when you don't know the answers

Your job is NOT to:

- Know everything about science and math
- Have perfect explanations for every question
- Create complicated lessons or activities
- Test your child's knowledge
- Make everything into a learning experience

The best STEM learning happens when children feel safe to explore, make mistakes, and ask questions. Your job is to create that safe space by being curious alongside them.

How to Use This Book

This book is designed to fit into your real life. You don't need to read it cover to cover. You don't need to remember everything.

This book is organized around the places where you already spend time with your child.

Here's how to make it work for you:

Start anywhere: Pick the chapter that matches where you spend the most time with your child or where you're most curious about learning opportunities.

Try one thing: Don't try to change everything at once. Pick one simple idea and try it for a week.

Follow your child: Pay attention to what interests your child most. Focus on those areas first.

Be patient: It takes time to develop new habits of noticing. Give yourself permission to learn gradually.

Keep it simple: The best STEM learning happens through simple observations and questions, not complicated activities.

You already spend time together. You already know your child better than anyone else. You already care about their learning and development. That's everything you need to get started.

This book will help you see that you're already doing so many things right. It will give you language for the learning that's happening. It will help you feel more confident in your ability to support your child's natural curiosity.

Your child is already learning from you every day. This book just helps you notice and celebrate what's already working beautifully.

Just remember you are already enough. Welcome to the amazing world of everyday STEM. It's been waiting for you all along.

Chapter 1: The STEM Mindset

When most people hear "STEM," they think about science class or math homework. They picture laboratories and textbooks. They worry about not knowing enough or getting the wrong answer.

But STEM in real life looks completely different. It looks like your child asking "Why does this happen?" It sounds like you saying "I wonder what would happen if we tried this."

Developing a STEM mindset isn't about becoming a different person or learning a lot of new information. It's about:

- Trusting your natural curiosity
- Believing that your child is already a capable learner
- Recognizing that everyday experiences are rich with learning
- Feeling confident in your ability to explore and discover together

Real STEM is:

- Noticing patterns in everyday life
- Asking questions about how things work
- Trying different solutions when something doesn't work
- Counting, measuring, and comparing things around you
- Building and fixing things together
- Observing changes and talking about what you see

School STEM often focuses on getting the right answer. Real-life STEM focuses on asking good questions and trying things out.

School STEM might say:

- "What is the correct answer?"
- "Follow these steps exactly."
- "Don't make mistakes."
- "You should already know this."

Everyday STEM says:

- "What do you think might happen?"
- "Let's try it and see what we learn."
- "Mistakes help us discover new things."
- "Nobody knows everything. We can figure this out together."

Your home doesn't need to be like school. Your home can be a place where curiosity leads to discovery, where questions matter more than answers, and where learning happens naturally through living.

Embracing "I Don't Know" Moments

The most powerful words in everyday STEM are "I don't know." When you say these words, you're not admitting failure. You're opening the door to discovery.

When Your Child Asks Questions You Can't Answer

What often happens: Your child asks "Why is the sky blue?" or "How does the microwave work?" You feel pressure to give a perfect explanation. You worry that saying "I don't know" makes you look uninformed.

What you can do instead: Say "I don't know. That's a great question. What do you think?" or "I'm not sure. Should we try to figure it out together?"

Why this works better:

- It shows your child that adults don't know everything, and that's okay
- It keeps your child's curiosity alive instead of shutting it down
- It makes you partners in discovery instead of teacher and student
- It takes pressure off you to be perfect

Making "I Don't Know" Into an Adventure

Instead of feeling embarrassed, try:

- "I don't know, but I'm curious too. What have you noticed?"
- "That's something I've always wondered about. Let's see what we can figure out."
- "I'm not sure, but you're asking really good questions."
- "I don't know the answer, but I know someone who might. Should we ask them?"

You can also:

- Wonder out loud together about possible answers
- Look for clues in what you can observe
- Try simple tests to see what happens
- Ask other people what they think
- Look things up together when you're both curious

Remember: Your child doesn't need you to know everything. They need you to care about their questions and be willing to explore together.

Building Your Confidence

Many parents worry they're not smart enough to help their children with STEM. But let me tell you the truth.

You use math when you:

- Figure out how much food to buy at the store
- Decide if you have enough time to run errands
- Measure ingredients for cooking
- Compare prices to find good deals

You use science when you:

- Realize that soap helps remove grease
- Understand that plants need water and sunlight
- Notice that hot water cleans better than cold water
- Know that ice melts when it gets warm

You use engineering when you:

- Fix things around the house
- Organize spaces to work better
- Find creative solutions to everyday problems
- Figure out how to assemble or install things

You use technology when you:

- Learn how to use new apps or tools
- Understand that different tools work better for different jobs
- Figure out why something isn't working
- Adapt to changes in how things work

You use STEM thinking every single day. You just call it "being a grown-up" or "common sense." You don't need textbook knowledge to help your child learn STEM.

If you enjoy cooking: Start noticing the science in your kitchen. Temperature changes, mixing reactions, and timing all involve STEM concepts.

If you like fixing things: Point out the engineering and problem-solving you do when you repair or improve things around the house.

If you're good at organizing: Show your child the math and systems thinking involved in organizing spaces and managing schedules.

If you enjoy being outdoors: Explore the science happening in nature during your regular outdoor activities.

Begin with what you already know and enjoy. Your confidence in familiar areas will grow into confidence in new areas. This practical knowledge is exactly what your child needs to understand how the world works.

Making STEM Feel Natural

The goal is not to turn every moment into a lesson. The goal is to help STEM thinking feel like a natural part of how your family approaches life.

If your child loves vehicles: Notice the engineering in cars, bikes, and trucks. Talk about how different vehicles solve different transportation problems.

If your child loves animals: Observe how different animals are designed for their environments. Notice how pets and wild animals solve problems differently.

If your child loves building: Point out the engineering in buildings, bridges, and structures around your community. Notice what makes some structures more stable than others.

If your child loves cooking: Explore the chemistry in food preparation. Notice how different ingredients behave and combine.

Your child's interests are the perfect starting point for STEM exploration. When children care about something, they naturally ask better questions and remember more of what they discover.

You don't need to be perfect. You don't need to know everything. You just need to be genuinely interested in the world around you and willing to share that interest with your child.

The Power of Everyday STEM

The most important thing you can teach your child about STEM is that it's interesting, accessible, and everywhere. When you approach the world with curiosity and openness, your child learns to do the same.

Trust yourself. Stay curious. The rest will follow naturally.

Miss Sierra

THE POWER OF EVERYDAY

STEM

Part II:

The STEM Method

I already
have what
it takes

Chapter 2: The S.I.E.R.R.A. Method

A Simple Way to See Learning Everywhere

Throughout this book, you've discovered STEM learning happening in every room of your house and every part of your day. But sometimes it helps to have a simple way to remember how to notice and support this natural learning.

The S.I.E.R.R.A. Method gives you six easy steps to turn any ordinary moment into a rich learning experience. You don't need to memorize complicated strategies. You just need to remember one word: SIERRA.

Simply **I**ncluding **E**veryday **R**eal **R**egular **A**ctivities

This method works because it uses what you already have, where you already are, and who you already are. No special preparation required. No extra time needed. No expensive materials to buy.

S - Simply

The first step is the most important: keep it simple. The best STEM learning happens through simple observations and natural conversations, not complicated activities or formal lessons.

What "Simply" Means

Simple doesn't mean easy or basic. It means uncomplicated and natural. The most profound learning often comes from the simplest moments.

Simple means:

- Using everyday language instead of scientific vocabulary
- Asking one good question instead of many questions
- Noticing one interesting thing instead of trying to see everything
- Following your child's natural pace instead of rushing
- Building on what your child already notices instead of directing their attention

The power is in the simplicity. One genuine observation or question opens the door to discovery better than ten forced educational moments.

Why Simple Works Better

Children respond to authenticity. When you're genuinely curious about something simple, your child feels that authenticity and becomes curious too.

Simple moments are sustainable. You can notice one interesting thing every day without feeling overwhelmed or running out of time.

Simple observations build on each other. Today's simple notice becomes tomorrow's deeper question. Learning grows naturally from these small seeds.

Simple feels safe. When there's no pressure to perform or understand complex concepts, children feel free to explore and ask questions.

I - Including

The second step reminds you that STEM learning works best when everyone is included. Your child isn't the student while you're the teacher. You're both explorers discovering things together.

What "Including" Means

Including means everyone learns together. You don't need to know the answers. You don't need to be the expert. You can be genuinely curious alongside your child.

Including means:

- Wondering out loud about things you notice
- Asking your child what they think
- Sharing your own observations and questions
- Learning from your child's discoveries
- Admitting when you don't know something

Why Including Works Better

It removes pressure. When you're learning together, your child doesn't feel like they need to perform or get the right answer.

It builds confidence. When children see that adults are still learning too, they feel confident that they can figure things out.

It creates genuine connection. Shared discovery brings families closer together than formal instruction does.

It models lifelong learning. Children see that curiosity and learning continue throughout life.

E - Everyday

The third step focuses on finding STEM in your ordinary, everyday activities rather than creating special educational moments.

What "Everyday" Means

Everyday means using your normal routines. The activities you already do contain rich learning opportunities. You don't need to add new activities to your schedule.

Everyday activities include:

- Making meals and cleaning up
- Getting dressed and ready for the day
- Running errands and traveling places
- Playing and spending time together
- Taking care of your home and belongings

Every single routine already contains multiple learning opportunities. The S.I.E.R.R.A. Method helps you notice them.

Why Everyday Works Better

It's sustainable. You can't run out of everyday activities, so you can't run out of learning opportunities.

It's relevant. Children care more about learning that connects to their real life than artificial educational activities.

It's efficient. You're learning during time you already spend together instead of finding extra time for formal instruction.

It's natural. Learning flows organically from life rather than feeling forced or artificial.

R - Real

The fourth step emphasizes using real materials, real situations, and real problems instead of artificial educational scenarios.

What "Real" Means

Real means authentic experiences. Instead of pretend activities designed to teach concepts, you use genuine situations that naturally involve STEM thinking.

Real experiences include:

- Actually measuring ingredients for cooking instead of playing with toy measuring cups
- Actually solving problems around the house instead of completing worksheets
- Actually observing weather changes instead of reading about weather
- Actually building and fixing things instead of using toy tools

When learning involves real materials solving real problems, children understand that STEM knowledge has genuine value in their lives.

Why Real Works Better

It matters. Children invest more energy in learning that has real consequences and real benefits.

It sticks. Learning connected to authentic experiences is remembered better than abstract lessons.

It transfers. Skills learned in real situations apply more easily to new real situations.

It motivates. Children see the immediate value of what they're learning when it solves real problems.

R - Regular

The fifth step reminds you that consistent, regular exposure to STEM thinking matters more than occasional dramatic activities.

What "Regular" Means

Regular means frequent, small doses. A few minutes of genuine curiosity every day builds stronger foundations than hour-long educational activities once a week.

Regular looks like:

- Noticing one interesting thing during each meal
- Wondering about one thing during each car ride
- Asking one good question during each play session
- Making one simple observation during each routine

Regular attention to STEM thinking creates habits that support lifelong learning.

Why Regular Works Better

It builds habits. Regular practice makes STEM thinking feel natural and automatic.

It creates momentum. Small, consistent steps forward add up to significant progress over time.

It reduces pressure. When STEM exploration happens regularly, no single moment needs to be perfect or comprehensive.

It develops fluency. Regular exposure helps children become comfortable with STEM concepts and confident in their own thinking.

A - Activities

The final step focuses on the activities you're already doing, recognizing that your current routines contain everything needed for rich STEM learning.

What "Activities" Means

Activities means your existing routines and natural play. You don't need to create new activities. You need to recognize the learning potential in activities you already do.

Your current activities already include:

- Household chores and maintenance
- Meal preparation and cleanup
- Transportation and errands
- Personal care and hygiene
- Recreation and entertainment
- Work and problem-solving

Every activity your family already does contains multiple STEM learning opportunities. The S.I.E.R.R.A. Method helps you see and support this natural learning.

Why Activities You Already Do Work Better

They're authentic. Your child engages more deeply with real activities than artificial educational activities.

They're complete. Real activities involve multiple STEM concepts working together naturally.

They're meaningful. Activities that serve genuine purposes hold children's attention better.

They're available. You always have activities you need to do, so you always have learning opportunities.

Using the S.I.E.R.R.A. Method

The beauty of this method is that you don't need to follow steps in order or use all six elements every time. Think of S.I.E.R.R.A. as a reminder checklist rather than a rigid procedure.

Quick S.I.E.R.R.A. Check

Before or during any routine activity, quickly think:

S - Simply: What's one simple thing I could notice or wonder about?

I - Including: How can I be curious alongside my child instead of teaching them?

E - Everyday: What learning is naturally happening in this routine activity?

R - Real: How is this authentic experience more valuable than pretend learning?

R - Regular: How does this moment build on yesterday and connect to tomorrow?

The Power of Everyday STEM

A - Activities: What STEM concepts are already present in what we're doing?

You don't need to think about all six elements every time. Even using one or two elements of S.I.E.R.R.A. will enhance the learning in any situation.

S.I.E.R.R.A. Examples Throughout Your Day

Bathtime S.I.E.R.R.A.: *Simply* notice how hot water steams while *Including* your child's observations about the bathroom mirror fogging up during your *Everyday* morning routine using Real steam from your *Regular* shower *Activity*.

Mealtime S.I.E.R.R.A.: *Simply* wonder how heat changes food while *Including* your child's predictions during your *Everyday* cooking routine using *Real* ingredients in your *Regular* meal preparation *Activity*.

Bedtime S.I.E.R.R.A.: *Simply* observe how shadows change when you turn off lights while *Including* your child's ideas about darkness during your *Everyday* bedtime routine using *Real* light sources in your *Regular* nighttime *Activity*.

Each application of S.I.E.R.R.A. feels natural because you're working with what's already happening in your life.

Remember This About S.I.E.R.R.A.

The S.I.E.R.R.A. Method isn't another thing to add to your to-do list. It's a way to see the incredible learning opportunities that already exist in your daily life.

You don't need to implement it perfectly. You don't need to use it every moment. You don't need to remember all six elements all the time.

S.I.E.R.R.A. is simply a tool to help you recognize that:

- Your **simple** observations matter
- **Including** your child as a fellow learner works better than teaching
- Your **everyday** routines are rich with learning
- **Real** experiences beat artificial educational activities
- **Regular** small moments build strong foundations
- Your current **activities** already contain everything needed for STEM learning

When you embrace the S.I.E.R.R.A. Method, you're not changing what you do. You're changing how you see what you do. And that changes everything.

Your everyday activities transform from chores into adventures. Your child's questions transform from interruptions into invitations. Your time together transforms from busy routine into rich learning.

S.I.E.R.R.A. helps you see that you're already doing everything right. You just needed a way to recognize it.

Miss Sierra

THE POWER OF EVERYDAY STEM

Part III:

The STEM Moments

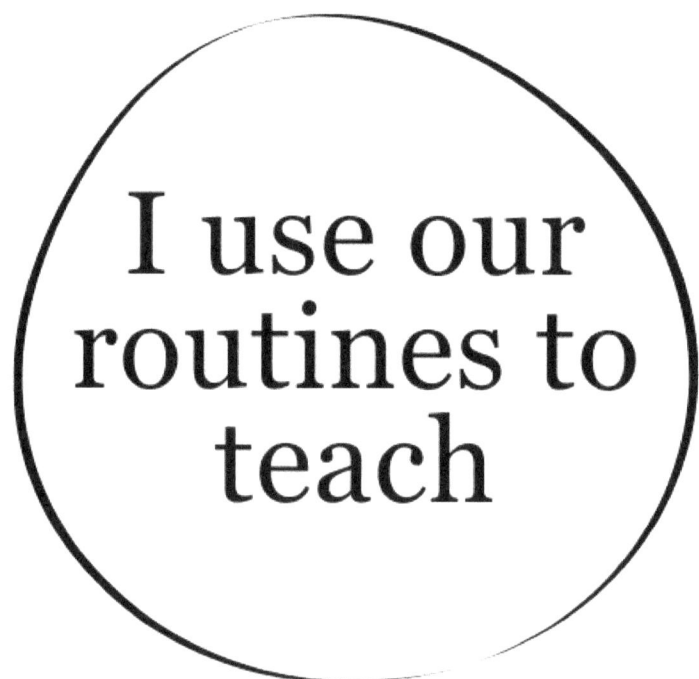

I use our
routines to
teach

Chapter 3: STEM in the Kitchen

You make breakfast. You wash dishes. You put away groceries. These simple tasks are already teaching your child science. You don't need to add anything new. You just need to notice what's already happening.

Let's look at what you're already doing and see the learning that's happening.

Kitchen Activity: Making Breakfast

Every morning, you make food. Your child watches. They're learning science without knowing it.

When You Cook Eggs

What you already do: You crack eggs. You cook them in a pan. They change from clear and runny to white and firm.

The science that's happening: Heat changes the eggs. This change can't be undone. Scientists call this a chemical change.

What to say:

- "Look how the egg changes when it gets hot."
- "The clear part becomes white."

- "What do you think makes it change?"

Let them help:

- Crack eggs into a bowl (they love this)
- Stir scrambled eggs
- Watch the changes happen

When You Make Toast

What you already do: You put bread in the toaster. Heat makes it brown and crispy.

The science that's happening: Heat takes water out of the bread. It also creates new compounds that make the brown color and good smell.

What to say:

- "The bread feels different now."
- "What changed?"
- "Why do you think it smells different?"

Let them help:

- Feel bread before and after toasting

- Compare light toast to dark toast
- Notice the smell changes

When You Pour Drinks

What you already do: You pour juice, milk, or water. Sometimes you add ice.

The science that's happening: Liquids take the shape of their container. Ice is solid water. It melts when it gets warm.

What to say:

- "The juice fits perfectly in the cup."
- "Watch the ice get smaller."
- "Where does the ice go?"

Let them help:

- Pour their own drinks (small amounts)
- Count ice cubes
- Watch ice melt in different places

Kitchen Activity: Cooking Dinner

Dinner time has even more science. Your child sees food change in many ways.

When You Boil Water

What you already do: You fill a pot with water. You put it on the stove. It gets hot and bubbles.

The science that's happening: Heat makes water molecules move faster. They escape as steam. The bubbles are water vapor.

What to say:

- "The water is talking to us with bubbles."
- "See the steam rising?"
- "What happens to the steam?"

Let them help:

- Watch for the first bubble
- See steam on the pot lid
- Feel the warm air above the pot (safely)

When You Mix Things

What you already do: You stir soup. You mix salad dressing. You combine ingredients.

The science that's happening: Some things blend together. Others stay separate. Oil and water don't mix well. Salt dissolves in water.

What to say:

- "Watch how these mix together."
- "Some things like to stay apart."
- "What happens when we stir?"

Let them help:

- Stir safe mixtures
- Shake salad dressing
- Watch ingredients combine

When You Use Heat

What you already do: You use the stove, oven, and microwave. Food changes when it gets hot.

The science that's happening: Heat changes food in many ways. It kills germs. It makes food softer. It creates new flavors.

What to say:

- "Heat is changing our food."
- "This will taste different when it's cooked."
- "Feel how much warmer this is."

Let them help:

- Compare raw and cooked vegetables
- Notice how cooking smells
- Feel warm dishes (safely)

Kitchen Activity: Storing Food

Putting food away teaches about preservation and temperature.

When You Use the Refrigerator

What you already do: You put some foods in the fridge. Others stay on the counter.

The science that's happening: Cold slows down germs and decay. Different foods need different temperatures to stay fresh.

What to say:

- "Cold helps food stay fresh longer."
- "Some foods don't need to be cold."
- "Why do you think milk needs to stay cold?"

Let them help:

- Put away refrigerated items
- Feel the difference between cold and room temperature food
- Notice which foods go where

When You Use the Freezer

What you already do: You freeze some foods. They get hard. They last much longer.

The science that's happening: Freezing stops most germs from growing. Water in food turns to ice. This preserves the food.

What to say:

- "Freezing stops food from going bad."
- "Feel how hard this is now."
- "Ice keeps food safe."

Let them help:

- Put items in the freezer
- Compare frozen and fresh versions
- Notice how freezing changes texture

Making Kitchen Activities Natural Every Day

The key is not to create special moments. The key is to notice the special moments that already exist.

Your kitchen is already full of learning. You don't need to become a teacher. You just need to become a noticer. Just start pointing out what you see. Your child will start seeing it too.

Your child learns by watching you work. They learn by helping with small jobs. They learn by hearing you think out loud about what you're doing.

You are already doing everything right. Start with one thing. Notice it together. Your kitchen science journey has already begun.

I create
learning
moments

Chapter 4: STEM in the Bathroom

Every day, you and your child use the bathroom. You wash hands. You brush teeth. You take baths. These simple routines are teaching physics without you even knowing it.

Water flows. Mirrors show reflections. Steam appears. Soap bubbles form. Your child sees all of this happening. They're learning about how the world works.

You don't need to turn bath time into school time. Your bathroom routines are perfect just as they are. Let's look at what's already happening.

Bathroom Activity: Washing Hands

Every time you wash hands, you see physics in action.

When You Turn on the Faucet

What you already do: You turn the handle. Water comes out. It flows down and around your hands.

The physics that's happening: Water pressure pushes water through pipes. Gravity pulls water down. Water takes the shape of whatever it touches.

What to say:

- "Water always flows down."
- "See how the water follows my hands."
- "The water changes shape."

Let them help:

- Turn the water on and off
- Cup their hands to catch water
- Watch water flow around their fingers

<u>**When You Use Soap**</u>

What you already do: You pump soap onto wet hands. You rub them together. Bubbles form.

The physics that's happening: Friction from rubbing creates heat. Air gets trapped in soap to make bubbles. Surface tension makes bubbles round.

What to say:

- "Rubbing makes my hands warm."
- "Look at all these tiny bubbles."
- "The bubbles are perfectly round."

Let them help:

- Make different sized bubbles
- Feel their hands get warm from rubbing
- Pop bubbles and make new ones

When You Rinse and Dry

What you already do: You rinse soap away with water. You dry hands with a towel.

The physics that's happening: Moving water carries soap away. The towel absorbs water through tiny fibers. Friction helps remove water.

What to say:

- "The water takes the soap with it."
- "The towel soaks up water."
- "Rubbing helps dry faster."

Let them help:

- Rinse their own hands thoroughly
- Feel how the towel absorbs water
- Try gentle rubbing versus patting dry

Bathroom Activity: Brushing Teeth

Even brushing teeth shows physics principles.

When You Squeeze Toothpaste

What you already do: You squeeze the tube. Toothpaste comes out in a line.

The physics that's happening: Pressure moves the toothpaste from high pressure to low pressure. The paste flows like a very thick liquid.

What to say:

- "Squeezing pushes the toothpaste out."
- "It comes out in the same shape as the opening."
- "Gentle squeezing works better than hard squeezing."

Let them help:

- Squeeze their own toothpaste (with guidance)
- See how different squeeze pressures change the amount
- Notice how the paste keeps its shape briefly

When You Brush

What you already do: You move the toothbrush back and forth. The bristles bend and spring back.

The physics that's happening: The bristles act like tiny springs. Friction helps remove plaque. The bristles store and release energy as they bend.

What to say:

- "The brush bristles bend and bounce back."
- "Gentle circles work better than hard scrubbing."
- "The bristles are like tiny springs."

Let them help:

- Feel how bristles bend on their finger
- Practice gentle brushing motions
- Notice how bristles spring back to shape

When You Rinse

What you already do: You swish water around your mouth and spit it out.

The physics that's happening: Moving water helps carry away debris. Momentum keeps the water moving in the direction you send it.

What to say:

- "Swishing moves the water around your teeth."
- "The water carries away what we brushed off."
- "Moving water cleans better than still water."

Let them help:

- Practice swishing gently
- Aim the water into the sink
- Feel how moving water works differently

Bathroom Activity: Taking a Bath

Bath time is full of amazing physics lessons.

When You Fill the Tub

What you already do: You turn on the water. The tub slowly fills up. The water level rises.

The physics that's happening: Volume and displacement work together. Water finds its level. Hot and cold water mix to make warm water.

What to say:

- "The water gets deeper as we add more."
- "Hot and cold water mix together."
- "The water stays flat on top."

Let them help:

- Watch the water level rise
- Feel the temperature change as you adjust
- See how adding toys changes the water level

When You Get in the Tub

What you already do: Your child gets into the water. The water level rises. Water may overflow.

The physics that's happening: Their body displaces water. The water has to go somewhere, so the level rises. This is the same principle that makes boats float.

What to say:

- "Look how the water rises when you get in."
- "Your body takes up space where water used to be."
- "The water moves to make room for you."

Let them help:

- Watch the water level before and after getting in
- Notice how different sized objects change water levels differently
- See how the water moves around their body

When You Play with Bath Toys

What you already do: Your child plays with cups, boats, and bath toys. Some float. Some sink.

The physics that's happening: Density determines what floats. Air inside toys makes them lighter than water. Heavy, solid things sink.

What to say:

- "Some things float. Some things sink."
- "The air inside helps it float."
- "Heavy things go to the bottom."

Let them help:

- Test different toys to see what floats
- Fill containers with water and see what happens
- Compare light toys to heavy toys

Making Bathroom Activities Natural Every Day

The physics is already there in every bathroom routine. You don't need to understand complex science. You just need to point it out.

Your child learns by watching daily routines. They learn by doing small tasks safely. They learn by hearing you notice interesting things.

Physics happens every time water flows. Science happens every time you adjust temperature. Learning happens every time you point out something cool.

You are already teaching perfectly. Just start noticing the amazing physics that happens in your bathroom every day.

Chapter 5: STEM in the Living Room

Every day, you and your child spend time in your living room. You watch TV together. You play with toys. You read books. You clean up and organize things. These everyday moments are teaching STEM without you trying.

Light comes through windows. Sounds travel around the room. Objects balance and fall. Remote controls send invisible signals. Your child sees all of this happening naturally.

You don't need to change what you do. The learning is already built into your daily life. You just need to notice it happening.

Starting with Your Normal Day

Your living room routines are already perfect for learning. Every activity shows your child how the world works. Let's look at what's already there.

Simple Ways to Notice Learning:

- Talk about what you both see happening
- Point out interesting things as they occur
- Use simple words to describe what you notice
- Let them help with safe tasks

- Be curious about everyday things together

Remember: You already see these things every day. Now you'll help your child see them too.

Living Room Activity: Controlling the TV and Remote

When you watch TV together, technology is working all around you.

When You Use the Remote Control

What you already do: You point the remote at the TV and press buttons. The TV changes channels or gets louder.

The science that's happening: The remote sends invisible light signals to the TV. These infrared signals carry information. The TV receives the signals and follows the commands.

What to say:

- "The remote talks to the TV with invisible light."
- "I have to point it at the TV to work."
- "The signal travels across the room."

Let them help:

- Hold the remote and press buttons (when appropriate)
- Try pointing the remote in different directions
- Notice that the remote works better when pointing at the TV

When You Adjust the Volume

What you already do: You make the TV louder or quieter with the remote.

The science that's happening: Sound waves travel through the air. Louder sounds make bigger waves. Your ears detect these vibrations.

What to say:

- "Loud sounds make big waves in the air."
- "Quiet sounds make small waves."
- "The sound travels from the TV to our ears."

Let them help:

- Listen to different volume levels
- Notice how sound fills the room
- Feel vibrations from loud sounds (like bass in music)

When Light Changes in the Room

What you already do: You turn lights on and off. You open and close curtains. The room gets brighter or darker.

The science that's happening: Light travels in straight lines. It bounces off objects to help us see them. More light sources make the room brighter.

What to say:

- "Light helps us see everything in the room."
- "Light bounces off things so we can see them."
- "More light makes the room brighter."

Let them help:

- Turn light switches on and off
- Open and close curtains
- Notice how shadows change when light changes

Living Room Activity: Cleaning and Organizing

Tidying up teaches classification and systems thinking.

When You Sort Toys

What you already do: You put toys away in different containers or areas. Books go with books. Blocks go with blocks.

The science that's happening: Classification helps organize information. Grouping similar things together creates systems. Systems make finding things easier.

What to say:

- "Things that are alike go together."
- "Sorting makes it easier to find things."
- "Everything has its own place."

Let them help:

- Sort toys by type, color, or size
- Put books back on shelves
- Make different groups and talk about why they go together

When You Vacuum or Dust

What you already do: You clean surfaces and floors with different tools.

The science that's happening: Static electricity makes dust stick to surfaces. Suction pulls dirt into the vacuum. Microfiber cloths use tiny fibers to trap dust.

What to say:

- "Dust sticks to things because of invisible forces."
- "The vacuum sucks air and dirt into the bag."
- "Different tools work better for different jobs."

Let them help:

- Dust safe surfaces with cloths
- Watch how vacuum suction works
- See how different tools clean different things

When You Arrange Furniture

What you already do: You move chairs, adjust pillows, or rearrange items to make the room comfortable.

The science that's happening: Heavy objects are harder to move. Friction makes sliding difficult. Leverage helps move heavy things with less force.

What to say:

- "Heavy things are harder to push."
- "Smooth floors make moving easier."
- "Lifting one end makes heavy things easier to move."

Let them help:

- Help push light furniture (safely)
- Notice which things are easy or hard to move
- See how lifting one end helps slide heavy objects

Living Room Activity: Playing with Toys

Toy time is full of physics lessons happening naturally.

When Toys Fall Down

What you already do: Toys fall off tables, couches, or out of your child's hands. You pick them up.

The physics that's happening: Gravity pulls everything toward the ground. Heavier objects don't fall faster than lighter ones in air. All objects fall at the same rate.

What to say:

- "Everything falls down, never up."
- "Gravity pulls things to the floor."
- "Heavy things and light things fall together."

Let them help:

- Drop different toys safely and watch them fall
- Notice that everything falls down
- Pick up fallen toys together

When You Build with Blocks

What you already do: Your child stacks blocks or other toys. Sometimes the stack falls over.

The physics that's happening: Balance depends on the center of gravity. Wide bases are more stable. Higher stacks are harder to balance.

What to say:

- "Wide bottoms help towers stand up."
- "Tall towers are harder to balance."
- "Everything needs support to stay up."

Let them help:

- Try building different shaped stacks
- See which designs stay up longer
- Notice what makes towers fall over

When You Roll Balls

What you already do: You roll balls across the floor. They slow down and stop.

The physics that's happening: Friction between the ball and floor slows it down. Smooth surfaces make less friction. Rough surfaces make more friction.

What to say:

- "The ball slows down because the floor rubs against it."
- "Smooth floors let balls roll farther."
- "Carpet stops balls faster than hard floors."

Let them help:

- Roll balls on different surfaces
- Compare how far balls go on carpet versus hard floor
- Push balls with different amounts of force

Making Living Room Activities Natural Every Day

The learning is already built into everything you do together. You just need to point it out as it happens.

Your living room is already a learning space. You don't need special educational toys or activities. You don't need to know complex science.

Your child learns by living daily life with you. They learn by helping with small tasks. They learn by hearing you notice interesting things happening around you.

You are already providing rich learning experiences. Just start pointing out the amazing things that happen in your living room every day.

Start with whatever your child notices first. Build on their curiosity. Your living room learning adventure is happening right now.

Chapter 6: STEM Outside

Every time you go outside with your child, you enter a natural classroom. You walk to the car. You check the mail. You water plants. You play in the yard. These simple outdoor moments are teaching STEM all around you.

The sun warms your face. Wind moves leaves. Water flows down drains. Birds fly overhead. Your child notices all of this happening naturally.

You don't need to plan nature lessons. The learning is already there waiting for you. You just need to step outside and notice it together.

Starting with Your Daily Outdoor Routines

Your outdoor activities are already perfect for learning. Every step outside shows your child amazing science. Let's look at what's already happening.

Simple Ways to Notice Outdoor Learning:

- Point out things you both see and feel
- Talk about weather and seasonal changes
- Use everyday words to describe what's happening

71

- Let them explore safely
- Wonder about natural things together

Remember: Nature is the best teacher. You just need to pay attention to what's already there.

Outdoor Activity: Walking and Moving

Every time you walk outside, physics is working.

When You Walk on Different Surfaces

What you already do: You walk on sidewalks, grass, gravel, and other surfaces. Your child feels the differences under their feet.

The science that's happening: Different surfaces create different amounts of friction. Smooth surfaces are easier to walk on. Rough surfaces give better grip but require more energy.

What to say:

- "This sidewalk feels smooth under our feet."
- "Grass is bumpier and softer."
- "Gravel makes our feet work harder."

Let them help:

- Walk on different surfaces and notice how they feel
- Compare how fast they can walk on smooth versus rough surfaces
- Feel the textures with their hands (when safe)

When You Go Up and Down Hills

What you already do: You walk up driveways, steps, or small hills. Going up is harder than going down.

The science that's happening: Gravity makes going uphill harder and downhill easier. Your muscles work against gravity when climbing. Potential energy increases as you go higher.

What to say:

- "Going uphill makes us work harder."
- "Gravity pulls us down the hill."
- "We use more energy going up."

Let them help:

- Notice how their breathing changes going uphill
- Feel how gravity helps them going downhill

- Try walking up and down the same hill

When You Carry Things Outside

What you already do: You carry mail, groceries, toys, or tools. Some things feel heavier than others.

The science that's happening: Weight is the force of gravity on objects. Heavier objects require more force to lift. Distribution of weight affects how hard things are to carry.

What to say:

- "Heavy things are harder to carry."
- "This bag feels light today."
- "Carrying two small bags is easier than one big bag."

Let them help:

- Carry lightweight items safely
- Compare the weight of different objects
- Help distribute weight in bags or containers

Outdoor Activity: Planting and Growing Things

Your yard and neighborhood plants teach biology every day.

When You Water Plants

What you already do: You water flowers, grass, or garden plants. The water soaks into the soil.

The science that's happening: Plants need water to survive and grow. Roots absorb water from soil. Water travels up through the plant to leaves.

What to say:

- "Plants drink water through their roots."
- "Water travels from roots to leaves."
- "Plants need water to stay healthy."

Let them help:

- Help water plants with supervision
- Watch water soak into soil
- Compare plants that get water to those that don't

When You See Plants Change

What you already do: You notice when flowers bloom, leaves change colors, or grass grows taller.

The science that's happening: Plants respond to seasons and weather. Growth requires energy from sunlight. Different plants have different life cycles.

What to say:

- "Plants change with the seasons."
- "Sunlight helps plants grow."
- "Different plants grow at different speeds."

Let them help:

- Point out new flowers or leaves
- Compare plants in sunny spots to those in shade
- Notice which plants grow faster

When You See Seeds and Fruits

What you already do: You see dandelions, acorns, berries, or other seeds and fruits around your yard.

The science that's happening: Seeds contain baby plants and food for growth. Fruits protect seeds and help them spread. Animals help disperse seeds.

What to say:

- "Seeds have baby plants inside."
- "Fruits protect the seeds."
- "Animals help spread seeds to new places."

Let them help:

- Look for different types of seeds
- Notice where new plants are growing
- Watch animals eating berries or nuts

Outdoor Activity: Observing Animals and Nature

The creatures in your yard teach biology and behavior.

When You See Birds

What you already do: You notice birds flying, landing, or looking for food around your home.

The science that's happening: Birds have adaptations that help them fly and survive. Different birds eat different foods. Birds migrate or adapt to seasonal changes.

What to say:

- "Birds have special bodies for flying."
- "Different birds eat different foods."
- "Some birds stay here all year, others visit."

Let them help:

- Watch birds and notice their different sizes and colors
- See what foods different birds prefer
- Listen to different bird sounds

When You See Insects

What you already do: You see ants, bees, butterflies, or other insects around your yard.

The science that's happening: Insects have important jobs in nature. Bees pollinate flowers. Ants work together in colonies. Butterflies go through metamorphosis.

What to say:

- "Insects have important jobs in nature."
- "Bees help flowers make seeds."
- "Ants work together like a team."

Let them help:

- Watch insects safely from a distance
- Notice what insects are attracted to
- See how insects move differently from other animals

When You See Other Animals

What you already do: You might see squirrels, cats, dogs, or other animals in your neighborhood.

The science that's happening: Animals have adaptations for their environment. They need food, water, shelter, and space. Different animals are active at different times.

What to say:

- "Animals need food, water, and safe places to live."
- "Different animals are good at different things."
- "Some animals come out during the day, others at night."

Let them help:

- Observe animal behavior safely
- Notice what animals eat and where they live
- See how animals move and interact

Making Outdoor Activities Natural Every Day

The outdoor classroom is always open. Every step outside is a chance to learn together.

Your yard and neighborhood are full of natural learning opportunities. You don't need to plan special nature activities. You don't need to know the names of all plants and animals.

Your child learns by experiencing the outdoors with you. They learn by touching, feeling, and exploring safely. They learn by hearing you notice interesting things in nature.

Science happens when you observe weather. Biology happens when you watch plants and animals. Physics happens when you feel wind and see shadows.

You are already connecting your child to the natural world. Just start pointing out the amazing things that happen outside every day.

Start with whatever catches your child's attention first. Follow their curiosity.

I make daily
routines
meaningful

Chapter 7: STEM and Laundry

Every week, you do laundry. You sort clothes. You measure detergent. You watch clothes tumble and spin. You fold clean clothes. These regular chores are teaching STEM without you even knowing it.

Water mixes with soap. Heat helps cleaning. Machines use different motions. Fabrics absorb and release water. Your child sees all of this science happening during normal laundry day.

You don't need to make laundry into a school lesson. The learning is already built into this weekly routine. You just need to notice it while you work.

Starting with Your Laundry Routine

Your laundry process is already perfect for learning. Every step shows your child amazing science and math. Let's look at what's already happening.

Simple Ways to Notice Laundry Learning:

- Talk about what you both see and feel
- Point out changes that happen during washing and drying

- Use simple words to describe what you're doing
- Let them help with safe tasks
- Notice patterns and differences together

Remember: Laundry day happens regularly. This gives you many chances to notice the same science over and over.

Laundry Activity: Sorting and Classification

Before you even start the machines, math and science begin.

When You Sort Clothes by Color

What you already do: You separate dark clothes from light clothes. You put whites together.

The science that's happening: Colors are made of dyes that can transfer between fabrics. Dark dyes can stain lighter fabrics. Hot water makes dye transfer happen more easily.

What to say:

- "Dark clothes can share their color with light clothes."
- "We keep colors separate so they stay bright."
- "White clothes need to stay with other white clothes."

Let them help:

- Sort socks by color
- Put light and dark clothes in different piles
- Notice which clothes have the brightest colors

When You Sort by Fabric Type

What you already do: You separate delicate items from sturdy clothes. You handle different fabrics differently.

The science that's happening: Different materials have different properties. Some fabrics are stronger than others. Some need gentler treatment to avoid damage.

What to say:

- "This soft shirt needs gentle care."
- "Thick jeans can handle stronger washing."
- "Different materials need different treatment."

Let them help:

- Feel the difference between thick and thin fabrics
- Compare rough and smooth textures
- Help separate delicate items

When You Count and Measure

What you already do: You count items, measure detergent, and decide how full to make each load.

The math that's happening: Counting helps you track items and decide on load sizes. Measuring ensures you use the right amount of detergent. Estimation helps you fit clothes in machines.

What to say:

- "Let's count how many shirts we have."
- "This measuring cup helps us use just enough soap."
- "We need to make sure everything fits."

Let them help:

- Count socks and match pairs
- Help measure detergent with supervision
- Estimate whether more clothes will fit

Laundry Activity: Using the Washing Machine

The washing machine is full of physics and chemistry.

When You Add Water and Detergent

What you already do: You set the water temperature and add detergent. The machine fills with water.

The science that's happening: Hot water molecules move faster and help cleaning. Detergent molecules have two different ends that help lift dirt away from fabric. Water and detergent mix to create a cleaning solution.

What to say:

- "Hot water helps clean better than cold water."
- "Soap helps water grab onto dirt."
- "The soap and water mix together to make a cleaning solution."

Let them help:

- Feel the difference between hot and cold water (safely)
- Watch detergent dissolve in water
- See how soap makes water work better

When the Machine Agitates and Spins

What you already do: You start the machine and it moves clothes around in different ways.

The physics that's happening: Agitation creates friction that helps loosen dirt. Spinning uses centrifugal force to push water out of clothes. Different motions serve different purposes.

What to say:

- "The machine moves clothes around to help clean them."
- "Spinning pushes water out of the clothes."
- "Different movements do different jobs."

Let them help:

- Listen to different sounds the machine makes during different cycles
- Watch clothes move through the machine window (if available)
- Notice how the machine changes what it's doing

When Water Drains Out

What you already do: Dirty water drains out and clean water rinses the clothes.

The science that's happening: Gravity pulls dirty water down and out of the machine. Fresh water rinses away remaining soap and dirt. Multiple rinses ensure clothes are clean.

What to say:

- "Dirty water flows out and down the drain."
- "Clean water washes away the soap."
- "We rinse more than once to make sure clothes are really clean."

Let them help:

- Listen for water draining out
- Notice when fresh water comes in
- Count how many times the machine rinses

Laundry Activity: Folding and Organization

Putting laundry away teaches geometry and organization.

When You Fold Clothes

What you already do: You fold shirts, towels, and other items to fit in drawers and closets.

The math that's happening: Folding creates geometric shapes. Different folding patterns use space more efficiently. Systematic folding makes stacks more stable.

What to say:

- "Folding makes flat shapes that stack nicely."
- "Different ways of folding use space differently."
- "Neat folds make stronger stacks."

Let them help:

- Fold simple items like washcloths
- Match corners and edges
- See how folding saves space

The Power of Everyday STEM

When You Sort by Size

What you already do: You organize clothes by size, type, or family member.

The math that's happening: Classification helps create order. Size relationships help determine storage needs. Systematic organization saves time later.

What to say:

- "Big clothes go with big clothes."
- "Everyone's clothes have their own space."
- "Organizing helps us find things quickly."

Let them help:

- Sort socks by size
- Put their own clothes in a separate pile
- Help organize items by type

When You Match Socks

What you already do: You find matching pairs and put single socks aside.

The math that's happening: Pattern matching helps identify pairs. Counting by twos shows even and odd numbers. Problem-solving helps find missing matches.

What to say:

- "Each sock needs its matching partner."
- "Two socks make one pair."
- "Sometimes we have to be detectives to find matches."

Let them help:

- Find matching pairs
- Count socks by twos
- Look for patterns and colors that match

Making Laundry Activities Natural Every Week

Laundry day becomes learning day when you notice the science that's already there.

Your laundry routine is full of learning opportunities. You don't need to make it complicated. You don't need to know complex chemistry.

Your child learns by helping with safe laundry tasks. They learn by watching you work through problems. They learn by hearing you notice interesting things during routine chores.

Chemistry happens when soap mixes with water. Physics happens when machines spin and tumble. Math happens when you sort, count, and measure.

You are already providing rich learning experiences every laundry day. Just start pointing out the amazing science that happens while you wash, dry, and fold.

Start with whatever part of laundry day interests your child most. Build on their natural curiosity. Your laundry learning adventure happens every week.

Chapter 8: STEM on the Go

Every time you leave the house with your child, you enter a world full of learning. You go to the grocery store. You visit the bank. You get gas for the car. You pick up prescriptions. These everyday errands are teaching STEM all around you.

Numbers appear on signs and screens. Machines sort and dispense items. People solve problems and make decisions. Your child sees all of this happening during normal trips around town.

You don't need to turn errands into field trips. The learning is already built into your regular stops. You just need to notice it while you're out and about.

Starting with Your Regular Errands

Your errands are already perfect for learning. Every stop shows your child how the world works. Let's look at what's already happening.

Simple Ways to Notice Learning on Errands:

- Point out numbers, patterns, and systems you see
- Talk about how different machines and processes work

- Use simple words to describe what's happening around you
- Let them help with safe tasks
- Notice how people solve problems in different places

Remember: You're already observing all of this. Now you'll help your child notice it too.

On the Go Activity: Traffic and Navigation

Getting around town involves navigation systems and traffic management.

When You Follow GPS Directions

What you already do: You listen to turn-by-turn directions and follow routes on a map.

The technology that's happening: Satellites provide location information. Computers calculate optimal routes. Real-time data updates traffic conditions.

What to say:

- "Satellites in space help the computer know where we are."

- "The computer finds the fastest way to get where we're going."
- "It knows about traffic jams and suggests different routes."

Let them help:

- Watch the map change as you drive
- Listen for direction updates
- Notice when routes change due to traffic

When You Observe Traffic Patterns

What you already do: You navigate through intersections, follow traffic signals, and merge with other vehicles.

The systems that's happening: Traffic signals coordinate vehicle flow. Road design manages traffic safely and efficiently. Driver behavior follows predictable patterns.

What to say:

- "Traffic lights help everyone take turns safely."
- "Road designers planned these streets to help traffic flow."

- "Following rules helps everyone get where they need to go."

Let them help:

- Count cars at intersections
- Predict when lights will change
- Notice patterns in how traffic moves

On the Go Activity: Grocery Store

Every grocery trip is full of math lessons.

When You Use a Shopping List

What you already do: You write down what you need and check items off as you find them.

The math that's happening: Lists help organize information systematically. Checking off items involves one-to-one correspondence. Planning ahead requires estimation and prediction.

What to say:

- "Our list helps us remember everything we need."
- "We can cross off each item when we find it."
- "Planning ahead saves us time and money."

Let them help:

- Help check items off the list
- Count how many items are left to find
- Look for items on the list

When You Compare Prices

What you already do: You look at price tags and decide which items give you the best value.

The math that's happening: Comparing numbers helps you find the best deals. Unit prices show cost per pound or ounce. Mental math helps you estimate total costs.

What to say:

- "This number tells us how much this costs."
- "We can compare prices to find the best deal."
- "Sometimes bigger packages cost less per pound."

Let them help:

- Point out price tags
- Find the lowest number when comparing similar items
- Help estimate whether you have enough money

When You Weigh Produce

What you already do: You put fruits and vegetables on scales and get price stickers.

The science and math that's happening: Scales measure the force of gravity on objects. Weight determines price for many items. Digital displays convert weight into cost automatically.

What to say:

- "The scale tells us how heavy these apples are."
- "Heavier items cost more money."
- "The computer figures out the price from the weight."

Let them help:

- Put items on the scale
- Watch the numbers change as you add or remove items
- Press buttons to get price stickers

On the Go Activity: Gas Station

Gas stations show engineering solutions and measurement systems.

When You Pump Gas

What you already do: You select fuel type, insert the pump, and watch numbers change on the display.

The engineering that's happening: Pumps use suction to draw fuel from underground tanks. Measuring systems track gallons dispensed. Safety systems prevent overfilling and vapor escape.

What to say:

- "Gas is stored underground and pumped up through hoses."
- "The machine measures exactly how much gas goes in our car."
- "Safety systems stop the pump when the tank is full."

Let them help:

- Watch the numbers change on the display

- Observe the pump handle and hose system
- Listen to the sounds that indicate when fueling is complete

When You Pay at the Pump

What you already do: You interact with payment screens and receipt printers.

The technology that's happening: Touchscreens respond to finger pressure. Card readers process payment information. Thermal printers create receipts without ink.

What to say:

- "The screen can tell where I'm touching it."
- "The printer makes words appear without using ink."
- "The computer remembers what we bought."

Let them help:

- Watch you use the touchscreen
- Take the receipt when it prints
- Notice how the screen changes based on your choices

Making It Natural During Every Errand

Every errand becomes a learning opportunity when you notice the systems, technology, and problem-solving happening around you.

Your regular errands are full of learning opportunities. You don't need to make special educational trips. You don't need to understand complex technology.

Your child learns by experiencing everyday business operations with you. They learn by watching systems work. They learn by hearing you notice interesting things during routine stops.

Math happens when you shop and pay. Science happens when you use technology. Engineering happens when you see efficient systems working.

You are already exposing your child to the working world every time you run errands. Just start pointing out the amazing systems and solutions you encounter every day.

Start with whatever interests your child most during your regular stops. Build on their natural curiosity.

I make a
difference

Conclusion: Your STEM Journey Continues

As you finish this book, take a moment to celebrate what you've discovered. You haven't learned how to become a STEM family. You've learned to recognize that you already are one.

This learning didn't start when you opened this book. It's been happening all along. Now you can see it clearly and celebrate it fully.

What You've Accomplished

You've learned to see STEM everywhere: From cooking breakfast to folding laundry, you now recognize the science, technology, engineering, and math woven into daily life. These aren't special activities you need to add to your schedule. They're opportunities you can notice and enjoy during time you already spend together.

You've built confidence in your ability to support learning: You don't need to be an expert to help your child discover how the world works. Your curiosity, life experience, and willingness to explore together are everything your child needs. When you don't know the answer, you've learned that "I don't know" is the beginning of an adventure, not the end of learning.

You've learned to follow your child's lead: Instead of worrying about covering specific topics, you've discovered the power of following your child's natural curiosity. Their questions guide your explorations. Their interests drive your discoveries. Their wonder keeps learning joyful and meaningful.

You've created a foundation that will last: The mindset you've developed will serve your family for years to come. As your child grows and their interests evolve, you'll be ready to explore new areas together. The habits of curiosity and observation you're building now will support their learning through school and beyond.

The most important thing you've learned is that small discoveries matter. You don't need dramatic experiments or breakthrough moments for learning to be valuable.

These moments happen dozens of times each day. Each one builds your child's confidence that they can figure things out, ask good questions, and understand how their world works.

You're not missing the important learning by focusing on small, everyday discoveries. You're building the foundation that makes all future learning possible.

Building Lasting Habits

The STEM mindset you've developed isn't just about childhood learning. You're modeling habits that will benefit your child throughout their life.

The habit of curiosity: When you wonder out loud about how things work, you show your child that learning never stops. Adult learners ask questions, seek answers, and remain open to new ideas.

The habit of observation: When you notice interesting phenomena during routine activities, you demonstrate the value of paying attention to the world around you. This observational skill serves scientists, engineers, artists, and problem-solvers in every field.

The habit of questioning: When you ask "What do you think?" and "What do you notice?", you show your child that their ideas matter. This confidence in their own thinking will serve them in school, work, and life.

The habit of persistence: When you try different approaches to solve problems around the house, you model resilience. Your child learns that challenges are normal and that creative problem-solving can overcome obstacles.

The habit of connection-making: When you help your child see relationships between different experiences, you're teaching them to think systematically. This ability to see patterns and connections supports learning in all subjects.

These habits extend far beyond STEM subjects. They support critical thinking, creativity, and problem-solving in every area of life.

Your Impact Extends Beyond Your Child

When you embrace everyday STEM learning, your influence reaches beyond your own family.

Your child becomes a STEM ambassador: Children who feel confident about science and math naturally share that enthusiasm with friends. Your child's positive attitude toward STEM learning influences their peer group.

You model inclusive STEM for other families: When other parents see your family enjoying STEM exploration together, they realize it's accessible to them too. Your example helps break down barriers that make STEM feel exclusive or intimidating.

You support your child's teachers: Children who come to school with strong foundations in curiosity, observation, and questioning are prepared to engage deeply with formal STEM instruction. Your everyday support amplifies what teachers can accomplish in the classroom.

You contribute to a more STEM-literate community: Citizens who understand basic STEM concepts make better decisions about technology, health, environment, and other issues that affect their communities. Your child's STEM literacy benefits everyone.

The Journey Continues

This book ends, but your STEM journey is just beginning. Every day brings new opportunities to explore, discover, and learn together.

Tomorrow morning, you'll make breakfast, and you'll notice the science happening in your kitchen with fresh eyes.

Next week, your child will ask a question you can't answer, and you'll say "I don't know. Let's figure it out together" with confidence.

Next month, you'll encounter a problem around the house, and you'll involve your child in the engineering process of finding a solution.

Next year, your child will face challenges in school, and they'll have the confidence to tackle difficult problems because they know they can figure things out.

Years from now, your child will make important decisions about their education and career with the foundation of confidence you're building today.

Every moment of curiosity, every shared discovery, every question explored together, contributes to this growing foundation. You're not just teaching STEM concepts. You're raising a confident, curious, capable human being.

You have everything you need to support your child's STEM learning. You have curiosity. You have daily routines. You have time together. You have love for your child and interest in their development.

You don't need to be perfect. You don't need to know everything. You don't need expensive materials or complicated activities.

You just need to notice the amazing world around you and share that wonder with your child.

STEM learning isn't something that happens later, somewhere else, with other people. It's happening right now, in your home, with your family.

Your everyday STEM adventure continues with every shared discovery, every question explored, and every moment of wonder you experience together.

Welcome to a lifetime of learning. The best is yet to come.

YOUR COMMUNITY PARTNER

Together we increase the confidence
and abilities of the children we love!

Mailing List

SIOHAN PRESS
A PUBLISHING COMPANY

Visit to download free resources
SiohanPress.com